Because You Are Polite
at the Dining Table

BY GINGER JOHNSTON PHILBRICK

BELLE ISLE BOOKS

Copyright 2015 by Ginger Johnston Philbrick. No portion of this book may be reproduced or transmitted in any form whatsoever without prior written permission from the publisher, except in the case of brief quotations published in articles and reviews.

ISBN: 978-1-9399302-1-7

Library of Congress Control Number: 2014942497

Published by

BELLE ISLE BOOKS
www.belleislebooks.com

Dedicated to my beloved parents,
Joseph and Edna Crallé Johnston,
who taught by example.

When you are polite,
others often invite you
to join them for fun
in the day and at night.

If you learn what is right,
and then frequently try it,
you will find you are liked
because you are polite.

Whether dining with two,

three,

four, or more,

you'll discover the meal is more pleasant . . .

. . . when you use your good manners in all that you do,
be the main course a pizza . . . or pheasant.

Oh, the food smells so good that you think you can't wait
for the others to sit down and eat it.
But *because you're polite*, you wait by your chair
till you see that your hostess is seated.

Then please have a seat, pull your chair up a bit,
and stay quietly at your own place,

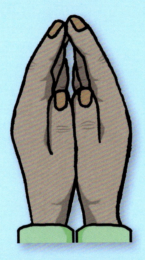

waiting to see what your hostess will do;
there may be a blessing or grace.

If your napkin is small, unfold it all.
If it's large, you should fold it in half.

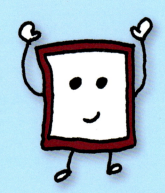

Because you're polite, you do all that you can
to keep it on TOP of your lap.

Because you're polite, you want to be part
of the many good times at the table.
So sit straight in your chair, pay close attention,
and be just as still as you're able.

Because you're polite, you know that the table
is not where your elbows should rest.
Just suppose that your elbow feels warm and you see
that it's in the cream soup of a guest!

—YUCK!

Though the meal is sooooo good,
and the temptation is there to eat it as fast as you can,
chew slowly and try to enjoy every bite,
because that is your hostess's plan.

Your hostess is always your guide at a meal
and will keep things from being confusing.
So please do not eat until she begins to,
and use the utensil she's using.

If you're served a new food without being asked
whether you'd like it or not,
because you're polite, you never let on
that you wish it were back in its pot!

Instead, why not try it? You're likely to find
it's not yucky, but actually tasty.
Your hostess will surely be pleased that you tried
. . . and you will be glad you weren't hasty.

If you would like butter to put on your roll,
but you see that it's out of your reach,
because you're polite, ask the one nearest to it,
"Will you pass me the butter dish, please?"

Chatting with others is certainly fun,
and we do it whenever we dine.
But gossip, gross stories, and terrible jokes
are quite rude and often unkind.

So *because you're polite*, talk of things that are pleasant:
vacations and hobbies and such.

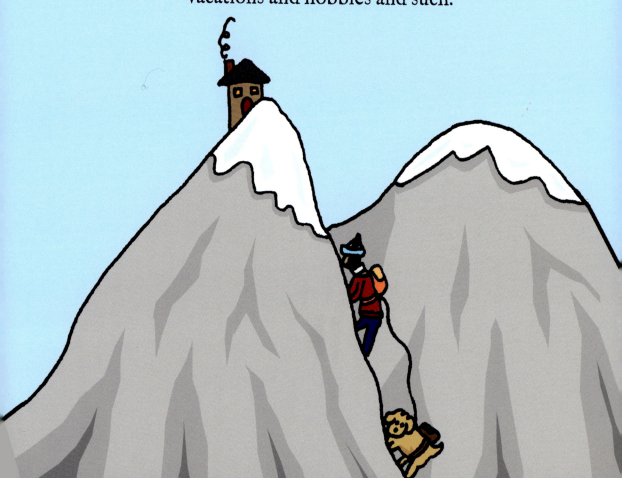

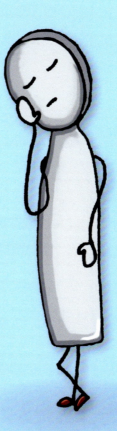

Whatever you do,
let the others talk too.

It's so
BORING
when
one
talks
too
much!

You may think the cake's great,
even better, in fact, than any you've tasted before.

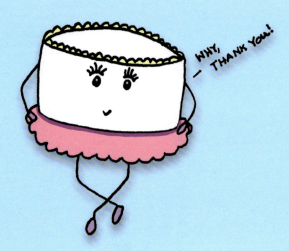

But *because you're polite*, you wait to be asked,
"My dear, would you care for some more?"

When the last crumb is gone and it's time to depart, your hostess would just love to hear...

...that you liked what she served and you had a good time. She'll respond, "Please come again, dear."

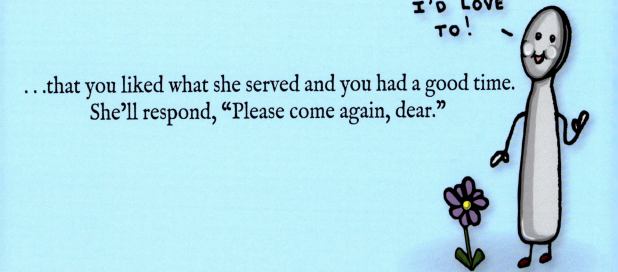

When you are polite, you'll be asked out at night or for luncheon, the zoo, or to help fly a kite.

It's a wonderful thing that can happen all right,
and all *because you are so very polite!*

OTHER TABLE MANNERS I KNOW:

1.

2.

3.

4.

5.